I
DECREE
AN
UNCOMMON
CHANGE

PASTOR (MRS) SHADE OLUKOYA

Chapter 1

I

Decree An Uncommon CHANGE

I Decree an Uncommon Change

Published - May, 2012

Pastor (Mrs) Shade Olukoya

ISBN 978-0692389409

© Battle Cry Christian Ministries

Published by:
The Battle Cry Christian Ministries
322, Herbert Macaulay Way, Yaba,
P. O. Box 12272, Ikeja, Lagos State, Nigeria.
Phone: 01 8044415, 0803-304-4239,
e-mail: sales@battlecryng.com
website: www.battlecryng.com

All the Scriptures are from the King James Version

Cover Illustration by: Sister Shade Olukoya

Printed In Nigeria.

Table of Contents

Chapter 1

I Decree An Uncommon CHANGE

Thou art my King, O God: command deliverances for Jacob. Psa. 44:4

Decrees are functions of power. It takes someone who exercises authority or power to come up with a decree. In the political realm, both civilians and military regimes often come up with laws. Such laws are binding on the entire citizenry.

Decree and laws are respected as there are stiff penalties for those who violate them. The truth, however is that, a decree cannot be made just by anyone. Absolute power belongs to God. He is the creator of heaven and earth. He is the God who is greater than the greatest, stronger than the strongest, richer than the richest and better than the most respected celebrity on earth.

The Bible refers to God as the Ancient of Days. He is the God of the whole earth. He is the Father of the fatherless, Husband of the widows.

THE OMNIPOTENT GOD

One of the passages that celebrate the greatness of the Almighty can be found below.

And I heard as it were the voice of a great multitude, and as the voice of many waters, and as the voice of mighty thunderings, saying, Alleluia: for the Lord God omnipotent reigneth. Rev. 19:6

The greatness of God determines the way He is celebrated. God is so great that, for Him to be celebrated requires a voice like the voice of a great multitude. It requires a voice that can be likened to the voice of a mighty thundering.

The omnipotence of God requires uncommon celebration. The Lord God omnipotent reigneth. What an awesome description. The name of God here highlights His unique attributes. The omnipotent God is the God who has all the power in heaven, on earth and under the earth.

The supreme power of God comes out in the term "omnipotent". We serve a God whose power is unlimited and whose power is unequaled. Absolute power belongs to God.

God hath spoken once; twice have I heard this; that power belongeth unto God.
Psa. 62:11

Power, strength, authority, equal resources and incomparable qualities belongs to God. If there is a major attribute of God that should be re-examined, it is the attribute of power.

THE LANGUAGE OF POWER

What is power? It is the ability to do something. Power can be described in many dimensions. But the power of God surpasses all power in every realm of life. God is the beginning, the source and the end of power. Every other power is inferior to the power of the Almighty. Since decrees are issued by powers and authorities, we can see therefore that God is the number one source of decrees. Hence, divine decrees are characterised by unchallengeable power. When God decrees, the whole of nature and all powers in the universe must take a bow and comply.

Governments of developed nations come up with decrees or instructions backed up by the political might of their nations. Those who default may bag jail terms, execution or the loss of certain rights and resources. That is how far earthly decrees can go. But when God decrees, people from all parts of the world are compelled to comply.

> *Thus saith the LORD, The heaven is my throne, and the earth is my footstool: where is the house that ye build unto me? and where is the place of my rest?* Isa. 66:1

The world of nature, as we all know today, has been established by a decree. Summer and winter are products of divine decrees. Seed time and harvest are divinely established to remain for life. Again, a decree has established the ordinance of day and night. Hence, no matter how long a night is, the dawning of a new day is inevitable.

> *While the earth remaineth, seedtime and harvest, and cold and heat, and summer and winter, and day and night shall not cease.* Gen. 8:22

The sky above your head has been held there by an eternal decree. Thunder, lightening, rain and the rainbow are also established by the decree of the Almighty. You can now see that God is the omnipotent and every power belong to Him.

INCOMPARABLE POWER

Governments come and go. Kingdoms rise and fall. Presidents are elected and they go out of office immediately their term expires. But, God remains the same. He is the only one whose throne never gets vacant. We often hear of coups and counter coups and elections of new presidents and the rise and fall of empires but God is above and over all.

The world has witnessed rulers like Mussolini, Winston Churchill, Napoleon Bonaparte, Adolph Hitler, Haile Selassie, Kwame Nkruma, Nelson Mandela, Leopard Sengor, Nnamdi Azikiwe and Idi Amin Dadda. But none of these rulers can be compared with the God who rules over heaven and earth.

> *And all the inhabitants of the earth are reputed as nothing: and he doeth according to his will in the army of*

heaven, and among the inhabitants of the earth: and none can stay his hand, or say unto him, What doest thou? Dan. 4:35

When we talk of decrees, we mean decrees backed up by the greatest power in the universe. God does not joke with power. He knows that no power can be compared with His power. Hence, He has proved to the whole world that His power is undoubtedly the greatest.

PRAYER POINTS

1. I render the weapons of my enemies useless, in the name of Jesus.

2. Let every weakness of my ancestors, the enemy is using against me, die, in the name of Jesus.

3. Every satanic conspiracy, to cage my destiny, scatter, in the name of Jesus.

4. Satanic strategy to delay me in the valley of life, die, in the name of Jesus.

5. Satanic wisdom, limiting my greatness, die, in the name of Jesus.

6. Satanic power, in my place of birth, manipulating my destiny, die, in the name of Jesus.

7. I refuse to enter into the grave the enemy has prepared for me, in the name of Jesus.

8. I refuse to become the wish of my enemy, in the name of Jesus.

9. Every voice of the enemy, over my life, be silenced by the power in the blood of Jesus.

10. Every evil arrow of the enemy, fashioned against my destiny, backfire, in the name of Jesus.

11. Let the camp of my enemies be baptized with confusion, in the name of Jesus.

12. Let God arise and let all His enemies in my life be scattered, in the name of Jesus.

13. By the power in the blood of Jesus, I claim victory over all the powers of my enemies, in the name of Jesus.

14. Every failure of my father's house, attacking my life, die, in the name of Jesus.

15. Every circle of problem in my foundation, die, in the name of Jesus.

16. Every manipulation of the evil powers of my father's house to lead me into error, die, in the name of Jesus.

17. Every evil word spoken, that is delaying my breakthroughs, scatter, in the name of Jesus.

Chapter 2

The
MYSTERY
of
transferred
POWER

T here is a mysterious similarity between God and His children. Just as the Almighty demonstrates power in a strange manner, His sons and daughters are also carriers of power. Hence, the Bible says.

Behold, I and the children whom the LORD hath given me are for signs and for wonders in Israel from the LORD of hosts, which dwelleth in mount Zion. Isa. 8:18

CONNECTED TO POWER

God has instituted a sort of change of ownership as far as His power is concerned. Of course, God has not relinquished His power but He has decided to share power with His sons and daughters. Hence He declared that His children are for signs and wonders. Signs and wonders take place through divine programmes which are occasioned by decrees.

In the society, the son of a president, a governor or a prince or a princess in a local environment are normally carriers of power. God has gone beyond that level by anointing everyone who belongs to Him with awesome power. The spiritual transfer of power has been backed up by a decree, here is the decree.

> *But as many as received him, to them gave he power to become the sons of God, even to them that believe on his name:* John 1:12

The decree has been legally established. God has decreed that anyone who becomes His son or daughter by right of conversion must automatically become heirs of His power. Power to become the sons of God is not just an ordinary power, it contains rights, privileges and authority to issue decrees.

The only way we can understand this is by meditating upon the depths, heights and extent of the awesome power of God and why God has decided to share the same quality of power with His beloved children.

TRANSFERRED POWER

Herein lies the mystery of transferred power which had not been exercised among sons and daughters of men. He came and shed His precious blood in order to seal the act of transferring the power. Initially, the disciples did not know what Jesus meant.

> *Verily, verily, I say unto you, He that believeth on me, the works that I do shall he do also; and greater works than these shall he do; because I go unto my Father.* John 14:12

None of the disciples believe that they could do greater works but the words of Jesus were very deep. He told the disciples He was going back to the Father. They did not know that they had made a conference among the trinity. The agenda of the conference was unlimited transfer of power. He was therefore going back to the Father to ensure that we would remain connected to the same quality of power which God had demonstrated.

Of course, it takes that kind of quality to do the greater works which Jesus promised. The disciples felt what Jesus was saying appeared too good to be true. So, he had to remind them that in the programme of the Almighty, beneficiaries of power transfer are supposed to be mini gods.

> *I have said, Ye are gods; and all of you are children of the most High.* Psa. 82:6

Jesus answered them, Is it not written in your law, I said, Ye are gods? John 10:34

MYSTERY DEMYSTIFIED

Ye are gods! What a mystery! What can we learn from here? Since, God rules by decrees, we are also supposed to rule by decrees. Jesus went further to expand on these when he taught on the power of attorney.

And I will give unto thee the keys of the kingdom of heaven: and whatsoever thou shalt bind on earth shall be bound in heaven: and whatsoever thou shalt loose on earth shall be loosed in heaven. Matt. 16:19

The word bind, here, connotes coming up with a decree. This is wonderful. Here, God tells you that you have been endowed by God to issue decrees throughout the whole earth. You can therefore decree anything into existence in Africa, Europe, America, Asia and it shall be established unto you. This shows you the extent of a divine decree. God is wonderful.

17

PRAYER POINTS

1. Every satanic sacrifice, carried out against my life, backfire, in the name of Jesus.

2. Every arrow of darkness, fired into my life, backfire, in the name of Jesus.

3. Evil altar in my foundation, attacking my life, catch fire, in the name of Jesus.

4. Every yoke of failure in my life, break into pieces, in the name of Jesus.

5. Every satanic agent, stealing from my life, be exposed and be disgraced, in the name of Jesus.

6. Evil walls, standing between me and my breakthroughs, collapse, in the name of Jesus.

7. I refuse to die unfulfilled, in the name of Jesus.

8. Every foundational backwardness, of my father's house, attacking my life, die, in the name of Jesus.

9. Every satanic curse, issued against my breakthroughs, break by the power in the blood of Jesus.

Chapter 3

How To
ENFORCE
a
DIVINE
DECREE

Thou shalt also decree a thing, and it shall be established unto thee: and the light shall shine upon thy ways. Job 22:28

God has positioned you to decree anything. God has placed awesome authority in your hands. Therefore, there is nothing you cannot decree. Here is how it works. You can decree something here on earth. The legislative officers of heaven ensure that the things you decree would be established unto you. This shows that, there is a legal department in heaven where decrees are put in black and white. There is also another department where the decrees are enforced. This picture is painted vividly below.

Let the high praises of God be in their mouth, and a twoedged sword in their hand; To execute vengeance upon the heathen, and punishments upon the people; To bind their kings with chains, and their nobles with fetters of iron; To execute upon them the judgment written: this honour have all his saints. Praise ye the LORD. Psa. 149:6-9

LAW ENFORCEMENT AGENTS

Immediately the law enforcement agents swing into action, you are automatically endowed with the power of execution here on earth.

I want you to close your eyes and make these powerful confessions.

- God had deposited awesome power within me

- I shall decree a thing and it shall be established.

> *For verily I say unto you, That whosoever shall say unto this mountain, Be thou removed, and be thou cast into the sea; and shall not doubt in his heart, but shall believe that those things which he saith shall come to pass; he shall have whatsoever he saith.* Mark 11:23

This passage further expounds the mystery of transferred power and authority.

> *For verily I say unto you, That whosoever shall say unto this mountain, Be thou removed, and be thou cast into the sea; and shall not doubt in his heart, but shall*

21

believe that those things which he saith shall come to pass; he shall have whatsoever he saith. Therefore I say unto you, What things soever ye desire, when ye pray, believe that ye receive them, and ye shall have them. Mark 11:23-24

You need decrees whenever a mountain stands between you and your destiny. You need decrees when you face challenges. You need decrees when the enemy wants to place stumbling blocks between you and your breakthroughs.

LEVELS OF PRAYER

There are prayers and there are prayers. There are various levels of praying, powered by various levels of authority. A child in the family, for example, can make a request. The mother will surely make a stronger request. But when the father comes up with a request, he comes with a great authority and power. But, that is how far the head of a home can go.

The head of a community has a greater level of power. When he comes up with an order, it is backed up by a greater power. We can move up from that to the level of a state governor, when he comes up on the radio to declare "Dear citizens, from now on I declare a state of emergency, I hereby impose a curfew from 6:00p.m. to 6:00a.m". Nobody will flout the decree. People would stay indoors, the moment it is 5:30p.m. But it can only cover a state. We can move up to the level of the president of a whole nation. When he imposes a curfew backed up by a decree, over 100 million people will be affected. Soldiers and police officers would be at alert nation-wide to enforce the decree. But when the King of kings and Lord of lords issues a decree, 7.2 billion people will be affected.

DIVINELY POSITIONED

Do you know that you have been divinely positioned to issue decrees that can affect more people that the president of your nation. This is the power given to you to make a decree. So when you stand up to say "I decree a change", no power on earth or hell can counter your words.

It is unfortunate that although, we are wielders of power, commanders of authority and men and women whose words is law universal, we often live timid lives, not knowing who we are in Christ.

If Jesus could say that we would do greater works than He did, why must we go about with fear and low self esteem? Would you ever expect a governor, king or president to go on air and be saying 'Citizens I know I don't have any authority, I just want to beg you to listen to my words. This state or nation belongs to all of us. I want you to do this or that but you are free to reject my words because I do not have any right over you. You have only elected me as a ceremonial leader"?

Let any leader speak like that, people would switch off their gadgets. Kings are not timid. Governors do not beg. Presidents do not tell people they can do what they like. Kings and leaders rule by edicts, decrees and laws that are embedded in the constitution or gazettes edicts.

YOUR AUTHORITY

Ordinarily, we are expected to manifest faith, but when we consider the issue of decrees, none of us can afford to joke with our authority. A decree is stronger than a promise. Those who have authority demonstrate it by coming up with decrees.

PRAYER POINTS

1. Any evil sacrifice manipulating my fruitfulness, catch fire, in the name of Jesus.

2. Satanic altar, attacking my breakthroughs, receive the thunder of God and scatter, in the name of Jesus.

3. Every evil personality, using the night to pollute my life, I cut off your head, in the name of Jesus.

4. Any evil power, claiming right to my breakthroughs, fall down and die, in the name of Jesus.

5. Any power, from the pit of hell, killing my breakthroughs, be devoured by the Lion of Judah, in the name of Jesus.

6. I release the blood of Jesus into my career, in the name of Jesus.

7. Every spirit of the tail, trying me down in the valley of poverty, die, in the name of Jesus.

8. Every foundational poverty of my father's house, my destiny is not your candidate, release me and die, in the name of Jesus.

9. Every circle of hardship, in my foundation, release me and die, in the name of Jesus.

10. Every blockage working against my breakthroughs, scatter, in the name of Jesus.

11. I withdraw my name from the book of failure, in the name of Jesus.

12. I withdraw my name from the book of poverty, in the name of Jesus.

13. Every evil power, discouraging my helper, loose your power, in the name of Jesus.

14. I refuse to be a beggar in the market of life, in the name of Jesus.

15. By fire, by thunder, I possess all my possession in the warehouse of Satan, in the name of Jesus.

16. I arise and shine, in the name of Jesus.

17. Wherever I go, favour shall follow me, in the name of Jesus.

18. I will never be rejected in my place of blessings, in the name of Jesus.

Chapter 4

The
POWER
of a
DECREE

What then is a decree? A decree is an official command. It is law. The government cannot hold a conference asking people's suggestion before a decree is promulgated. To decree is to establish a thing militantly. When authorities come up with decrees, they do so with boldness without any apology. They do not care whose ox is gored. It is a decision issued by the powers that be, locally or internationally.

It is therefore, an official order no one can challenge. We need to take a second look at the military aspect of our son-ship. The Bible tells us that God rules "in the army of heaven". This shows that heaven is our military headquarters, God is our All in All and Jesus is our generalissimo or commander-in-chief.

SOLDIERS OF CHRIST

Christianity is not a democratic setup, it is highly military; by the act of salvation, we are soldiers of Christ,

> *Thou therefore endure hardness, as a good soldier of Jesus Christ. No man that warreth entangleth himself with the affairs of this life; that he may please him who hath chosen him to be a soldier.*
> 2Tim. 2:3-4

For quite a long time, we have lost sight of the military side of Christianity. As a child of God, you are not a weakling. God has put upon you the garment of authority with which you can issue military decrees.

It is amazing that it is only believers that can decree governments in and out of office. We are the only ones who can install local government chairmen, governors and presidents. Just give me a few prayer warriors in a local government or a state and the prayer squad will pray any government in and out of power. It is not only through the ballot box that political leaders can be voted, prayer is stronger than the ballot box.

SPIRITUAL KING MAKERS

We only need intercessors and prayer warriors who vow that they will not eat until good governance is achieved. Such people would become the people who will move the hand of God and determine those who sit in government houses.

We live in an era where genuine Christians will come together and determine the type of government they want. A time will come in nations, when people would realize that the authority which believers have is strong enough to affect whole nations and communities.

The kind of decree you can come up with would surely affect political leaders, military, professionals, the elite class, Christian and Muslim community, different people, groups and tribes.

Decree will work for both male and female, young and old, poor and rich and every cadre of the society. Such power and authority is awesome. We need to wield such power and make use of our authority today. God has invested so much upon our lives. It is wrong for a child of God who has been given great power and authority to go about crying and begging. Of what use is power when you cannot use it?

It does not get anything done? Let me share this great truth with you. God has paid a great price to make us kings. He did not spare any effort when he declared that we are men and women of authority. The Bible makes it clear that, he has made and established us as kings unto Himself.

30

And hath made us kings and priests unto
God and his Father; to him be glory and
dominion for ever and ever. Amen.
Rev. 1:6

What a great privilege to be made a king by the One who
alone has unparalleled power.

Which in his times he shall shew, who is
the blessed and only Potentate, the King
of kings, and Lord of lords; Who only
hath immortality, dwelling in the light
which no man can approach unto; whom
no man hath seen, nor can see: to whom
be honour and power everlasting. Amen.
1Tim. 6:15-16

31

PRAYER POINTS

1. Every blockage standing between me and my helper, collapse and scatter, in the name of Jesus.

2. Every satanic odour, chasing away my divine helper, disappear, in the name of Jesus.

3. Anything whatsoever, magnetizing the wrong people to my life, catch fire, in the name of Jesus.

4. Every connection between me and the spirit of anti-greatness, die, in the name of Jesus.

5. Garments of stagnation, covering my greatness, catch fire, in the name of Jesus.

6. Every evil dream, hindering my greatness, die, in the name of Jesus.

7. Every satanic power, rewinding the clock of my greatness, fall down and die, in the name of Jesus.

8. Every satanic delay to my greatness, scatter, in the name of Jesus.

9. I receive power and divine connection to be great, in the name of Jesus.

10. I receive opportunity of a lifetime, in the name of Jesus.

11. I reject Satanic breakthroughs assigned to divert my divine breakthroughs, in the name of Jesus.

12. Every door of opportunity, that the enemy has closed against my life in the time of ignorance, be opened by fire, in the name of Jesus.

13. All my helpers, receive power to help me, in the name of Jesus.

14. Let the door of worldwide breakthroughs be opened unto me, in the name of Jesus.

15. I receive breakthroughs of a lifetime, in the name of Jesus.

16. Every foundational rejection of my father's house, manifesting in my life now, die, in Jesus' name.

17. Every spirit of disfavour, loose your power upon my life, in the name of Jesus.

18. Every demonic personality, that has refused to let me go, die, in the name of Jesus.

Chapter 5

OUR *Kingly* RULE

If the one who has everlasting power and honour could share some of His power with you, why should you not demonstrate the awesome power that lies buried within you? Do you know this? We are kings. We are supposed to act and rule. We must demonstrate the fact that we are kings and queens of no mean status. We are not kings by selection, we are not kings because we are voted into any office by human beings. We are kings by divine appointment. We got this divine appointment through the instrumentality of the blood of Jesus. God is not known for half measures. Whenever he does anything, He does it to the point of completion.

The Bible says;

> *Moreover whom he did predestinate, them he also called: and whom he called, them he also justified: and whom he justified, them he also glorified. What shall we then say to these things? If God be for us, who can be against us?*
> Rom. 8:30-31

God has called, justified and glorified us. What type of glory are we talking about?

35

And the glory which thou gavest me I have given them; that they may be one, even as we are one: John 17:22

THE GLORY

The same glory that Jesus had is the same He has bestowed upon us by a divine fiat. We have been made to stand where Jesus stood and sit where He sat. Why did God do all this?

And hath raised us up together, and made us sit together in heavenly places in Christ Jesus: That in the ages to come he might shew the exceeding riches of his grace in his kindness toward us through Christ Jesus. Eph. 2:6-7

God wants to show the exceeding riches of His grace. He wants to demonstrate the riches and the extent of his programme for His children.

I want you to close your eyes and pray aloud this prayer point.

36

- *Father, in the name of Jesus, it is written in your word that I shall be the head and not the tail. Therefore, whatever I decree from now henceforth shall come to pass.*

A WONDERFUL POSITION

From the beginning of creation, it has been God's desire to grant unto man a position of dignity, a wonderful privilege and grace that is unfathomable. God created everything we would ever need before man was created. By the time God was going to create man, He did so in His own image. God's purpose was to accord unto man a position of dignity and a place of excellence.

If we survey the entire gamut of God's great plan for man, we will discover that we were never meant to play second fiddle.

> *O LORD our Lord, how excellent is thy name in all the earth! who hast set thy glory above the heavens. Out of the mouth of babes and sucklings hast thou ordained strength because of thine enemies, that thou mightest still the enemy and the avenger. When I consider thy heavens, the work of thy fingers, the*

37

moon and the stars, which thou hast ordained; What is man, that thou art mindful of him? and the son of man, that thou visitest him? For thou hast made him a little lower than the angels, and hast crowned him with glory and honour. Thou madest him to have dominion over the works of thy hands; thou hast put all things under his feet: All sheep and oxen, yea, and the beasts of the field; The fowl of the air, and the fish of the sea, and whatsoever passeth through the paths of the seas. O LORD our Lord, how excellent is thy name in all the earth!
Psa. 8:1-9

Just like God's name is excellent, God had excellence in mind when he made man. Satan, the enemy of man became infuriated. He came up with perfect hatred for man, sowed the seed of temptation and derailed the destiny of man.

As soon as the enemy rearranged mankind's destiny, he began to rejoice having made man lose a great privilege. Satan turned the divine purpose upside down and got mankind into trouble.

The position of headship glory and authority was lost by man. The devil is very wicked. Through the evil offer which he gave man, he introduced a demonic trade by barter. He sold a dummy to man and made man loose what is precious.

A SECOND CHANCE

Man lost the greatest possession and greatest offer ever made. It was a colossal loss. But thank God for mercy and grace. God gave man a second chance through the instrumentality of the offer of salvation. God could not watch man fall from grace to grass and remain in the valley of life.

> *For since by man came death, by man came also the resurrection of the dead. For as in Adam all die, even so in Christ shall all be made alive.* 1Cor. 15:21-22

God came up with the plan of redemption. Thus God has restored man to the original position. What we lost in Adam, the first man, has been restored in Christ, the second man.

And having spoiled principalities and powers, he made a shew of them openly, triumphing over them in it. Col. 2:15

This is the foundation for our decree. For you to issue a decree and demonstrate power and authority, God has to deal with the fake power paraded by the enemy. Jesus did not do this secretly. He publicly made an open show of the devil. He triumphed over the enemy in the full glare of the public. Jesus gave the devil a public disgrace. He gave satan what can be described as a technical knockout.

Lest any of us become afraid and begin to panic, the captain of our redemption paid for our salvation on the cross. He made a bold declaration saying; "It is finished"! This means that, our shame is finished, our sorrow is finished, our darkness is finished, our diseases are gone. Everything called backwardness is over. There is no area where the enemy can cheat us any longer. It is done. It has been concluded. The enemy has been paralysed. His works have been gathered together, finished and concluded.

PRAYER POINTS

1. Blood of Jesus, kill every evil mark on my body, in the name of Jesus.

2. Arrows of mistake and error, manifesting in my life in the presence of my helpers, die, in Jesus' name.

3. Any evil, done against my life, that is now making life difficult for me, die, in the name of Jesus.

4. Garments of disfavour, covering my glory, catch fire, in the name of Jesus.

5. Satanic incantation, working against my spirit-man, perish by fire, in the name of Jesus.

6. Any power, using my name against me, die, in the name of Jesus.

7. Any power in my father's house, using my date of birth against my destiny, die, in the name of Jesus.

8. Anointing for favour from above, break the yoke of disfavour in my life, in the name of Jesus.

9. I walk out of the bondage of disfavour, in the name of Jesus.

10. My heaven of favour, open now, in the name of Jesus.

11. Every visible and invisible blockage on my way to progress, catch fire, in the name of Jesus.

12. Every satanic immigration officer, manifesting in my dream, saying "no" to my fulfilment, die, in the name of Jesus.

13. I receive power from above to overcome every financial obstacle that is delaying my progress, in the name of Jesus.

14. Every satanic document, that the enemy is using against me, catch fire, in the name of Jesus.

15. You mistakes of the past, you will not destroy my testimony, in the name of Jesus.

16. Lord, open doors of opportunity to me through this prayer, in the name of Jesus.

17. Thank God for the name of Jesus.

Chapter 6

A GLORIOUS Plan

God's plan for mankind has remained a glorious one. God has never come up with a plan that has been less than glorious. The problem however is that, man has failed to cooperate with God.

Something tragic happened at the beginning of the story of mankind. The power to promulgate decree was lost through carelessness. The devil, the enemy of mankind, came with a subtle plan. He cleverly stole the authority and the power bestowed upon man. Sin came and man lost dominion.

A LOOPHOLE

The devil secured a loophole through Eve.

> *Now the serpent was more subtil than any beast of the field which the LORD God had made. And he said unto the woman, Yea, hath God said, Ye shall not eat of every tree of the garden? And the woman said unto the serpent, We may eat of the fruit of the trees of the garden: But of the fruit of the tree which is in the midst of the garden, God hath said, Ye shall not eat of it, neither shall ye touch it, lest ye die.*

*And the serpent said unto the woman,
Ye shall not surely die: For God doth
know that in the day ye eat thereof, then
your eyes shall be opened, and ye shall be
as gods, knowing good and evil. And
when the woman saw that the tree was
good for food, and that it was pleasant
to the eyes, and a tree to be desired to
make one wise, she took of the fruit
thereof, and did eat, and gave also unto
her husband with her; and he did eat.
And the eyes of them both were opened,
and they knew that they were naked; and
they sewed fig leaves together, and made
themselves aprons.* Gen. 3:1-7

Satan succeeded. He used the bait and the hook by
promising Eve that her eyes and that of her husband
shall be opened and they shall be as gods. The devil will
go any length in order to achieve his mission. He often
speaks what looks like the truth just to carry his victims
along. True, Adam and Eve needed the opening of their
eyes. They also needed to discover their status as gods.
Additionally they also needed to know good and evil.

45

The three offers which the devil gave them were not really bad in themselves.

> *For God doth know that in the day ye eat thereof, then your eyes shall be opened, and ye shall be as gods, knowing good and evil.* Gen. 3:5

TWISTED SCRIPTURES

The promises were scriptural. It is just that the devil became an angel of light that moment in order to twist the word of God. He appealed to principles that were correct. For example, the Bible says that we need the eyes of our understanding to be enlightened. Spiritual enlightenment is quite good. But the Devil was selling them a counterfeit rather than the genuine.

> *The eyes of your understanding being enlightened; that ye may know what is the hope of his calling, and what the riches of the glory of his inheritance in the saints,* Eph. 1:18

We need the eyes of our understanding to be enlightened but it has to be enlightened in the positive sense. We can get to a point where we have good spiritual understanding. Whatever we need to make our eyes opened can be found in the word of God. We must be very careful here as a lot of false religions and occult groups are trying to offer us esoteric or deeper knowledge which will land us at the same place where Adam and Eve landed.

MODERN CULTS

Modern cults may put up adverts telling those who are eager to know more about the deep things of life to try their counterfeit methods. You don't need such a demonic knowledge. Just read your Bible and meditate deeply on God's word and you will be filled with knowledge.

YE ARE GODS

The second thing which the devil offered is that, Adam and Eve would be as gods. Of course, you must have discovered by now that was what God offered. But there are two types of gods. There is a way you can be like your Father, God, by taking up His nature and character. In this regard, you are godly. So when Jesus said "Ye are gods", He simply meant that you are a little god. Just like Christians were so called in Antioch, you can be called a small god and an exact replica of your heavenly Father. The scriptures are clear.

And when he had found him, he brought him unto Antioch. And it came to pass, that a whole year they assembled themselves with the church, and taught much people. And the disciples were called Christians first in Antioch. Acts. 11:26

Be ye therefore followers of God, as dear children; Eph. 5:1

That ye may be the children of your Father which is in heaven: for he maketh his sun to rise on the evil and on the good, and sendeth rain on the just and on the unjust. Matt. 5:45

Be ye therefore perfect, even as your Father which is in heaven is perfect. Matt. 5:48

Be ye therefore merciful, as your Father also is merciful. Luke 6:36

One thing the devil does is that, he comes up with a counterfeit of every original thing God does. He promises those who follow him spiritual enlightenment but what he give is demonic enlightenment. He promises those who care to listen that they can be like God. But, what he offers is fake. While as believers we can truly be like our Father God, those who follow the devil will end up becoming demonic agents like their master, satan.

POWER OF DISCERNMENT

The third thing that the devil offered Adam and Eve is that they would receive the power of discernment. Again the power of discernment is real. It is one of the things taught in the scriptures.

> *To another the working of miracles; to another prophecy; to another discerning of spirits; to another divers kinds of tongues; to another the interpretation of tongues:* 1Cor. 12:10

> *But strong meat belongeth to them that are of full age, even those who by reason of use have their senses exercised to discern both good and evil.* Heb. 5:14

These passages show that God offers us the power of discernment. The devil has quickly gone ahead to offer his own kind of power of discernment. But the Bible has told us to refrain from such demonic knowledge.

But unto you I say, and unto the rest in Thyatira, as many as have not this doctrine, and which have not known the depths of Satan, as they speak; I will put upon you none other burden. Rev. 2:24

SATANIC OPPORTUNITIES

The mistake people make is to accept satanic opportunities rather than wait for the good offers which they stand to gain by following the way of God. The truth is that there is nothing we would ever need that God does not have in abundance. If Adam and Eve had waited for the unfolding of God's plan, they would have gained in a positive form, every fake thing that the devil offered. It was not just what the devil said that matter, but the carnal gain which Eve stood to make that captivated her.

And when the woman saw that the tree was good for food, and that it was pleasant to the eyes, and a tree to be desired to make one wise, she took of the fruit thereof, and did eat, and gave also unto her husband with her; and he did eat. Gen. 3:6

Adam and Eve accepted what the devil sold to them and their eyes got opened.

And the eyes of them both were opened, and they knew that they were naked; and they sewed fig leaves together, and made themselves aprons. Gen. 3:7

PRAYER POINTS

1. I paralyse, every activity of physical and spiritual parasites and devourers in my life, in the name of Jesus.

2. Powers denying me my due miracles, receive the stones of fire, in the name of Jesus.

3. I recover, all the ground that I had lost to the enemy, in the name of Jesus.

4. I bind the spirit of depression, frustration and disillusionment in my life, in the name of Jesus.

5. Heavenly surgeons, perform the necessary surgical operations in all the areas of my life, in the name of Jesus.

6. Lord Jesus, carry out all the repairs that are necessary in my life, in the name of Jesus.

7. Let all the parasites, feeding on any area of my life be roasted, in the name of Jesus.

8. Fire of God, consume the evil clock of the enemy that is working against my life, in the name of Jesus.

9. I command all the damages done to my life by
    .... *(pick from the underlisted)* to be repaired,
    in the name of Jesus.
    - evil tongue
    - demonic prophecies
    - witchcraft spells and curses
    - personal negative confessions
    - household wickedness

10. My life is not a fertile ground for any evil to thrive,
    in the name of Jesus.

11. I command all doors of good things, closed against
    me by the enemy to be opened, in Jesus' name.

12. I reject the spirit of impossibility, I claim open
    doors, in the name of Jesus.

13. *(Put in the area of your life you want)* I decree
    restoration seven fold in ..... area of my life, in the
    name of Jesus.

14. I refuse to wage war against myself, in the name
    of Jesus.

15. Lord, make my case a miracle. Shock my foes,
    friends and even myself, in the name of Jesus.

Chapter 7

Recover your AURA

Many young people today are searching for knowledge. They are running after discovering a lot of deep things. If you want to discover deep things in the kingdom of darkness, you will make such discoveries but at the same time, you will enter into a lifelong bondage.

The eyes of Adam and Eve were opened. Their eyes were opened to shame. Their eyes were opened to emptiness. Their eyes were opened to disgrace. Their eyes were opened to failure. Their eyes were opened to abandonment, their eyes were opened to being banished from the presence of God. Their eyes were opened to bondage. Their eyes were opened to satanic captivity, their eyes were opened to error. Their eyes were opened to problems.

WHAT A SIGHT!

Immediately they opened their eyes, they saw ignominy. They opened their eyes and beheld monumental captivity. When they opened their eyes, they beheld the works of the devil. When they opened their eyes, they discovered their nakedness. Unfortunately, the knowledge they had did not do them any good.

I have a word here for those who go to the camp of the devil to obtain power. Tell me, what will you do with the power? Will the power save you from death? Will the power make you to cast off the garment of mortality?

What Adam and Eve bought from the supermarket of the devil became useless. They paid for bondage. They paid for sorrow and sadness. They paid for fear. They paid for foolishness and the only thing they could do was to sow fig leaves together in order to cover themselves. What they paid for made them to run when they heard the voice of God. What an evil purchase! May God deliver us from going to the market to buy bondage.

THE UNTOLD STORY

My heart goes to women who go to the market to buy all kinds of trinkets and jewelleries without knowing the origin of such items. Most of the jewelleries which women use can be traced to the Far East. Unknown to such women, when such jewelleries an articles are manufactured, the craftsmen take them to the houses of their gods for dedication. After carrying out the rituals of demonic dedication, the items are sent to the market. People travel from African countries to places like

56

Thailand, Bankok and India to buy expensive jewelleries. The story that may not be told however is that, such jewelleries could be manufactured from the marine world and dedicated to powerful oriental idols.

Many of us would not want to go to the shrine of any idol for fear of being conscripted into bondage. But when you put on bangles and necklaces that are loaded with demons, you have followed the footsteps of Eve by paying for your own bondage.

The truth is that, no matter how powerful the devil was, he could not have forced Adam and Eve to accept his offer. He only made the offers and Adam and Eve fell for it.

My father in the Lord and my husband, Dr. Olukoya used to say that, the devil will enter into arguments with a lot of people. We lay every blame on the devil but the devil cannot carry you to the market, take money from your pocket or handbag and purchase bondage for you. We must call a spade a spade and own up to our mistakes rather than heap the blames on the devil.

THE SATANIC GAME

Adam and Eve gained nothing. They lost everything. They lost the beauty of the garden. They lost the presence of God. They lost the regular visits of God whenever He came visiting at the cool of the day. God had to come up with a plan of salvation and restoration. Jesus Christ shed His blood in order to institute a buyback for man in the slave market.

For since by man came death, by man came also the resurrection of the dead. For as in Adam all die, even so in Christ shall all be made alive. 1Cor. 15:21-22

And having spoiled principalities and powers, he made a shew of them openly, triumphing over them in it. Col. 2:15

Through the shed blood of Jesus Christ, the glory that was lost got restored.

But God, who is rich in mercy, for his great love wherewith he loved us, Even when we were dead in sins, hath

*quickened us together with Christ,
And hath raised us up together, and
made us sit together in heavenly places
in Christ Jesus:* Eph. 2:4-6

God effected a change and restoration to His original intention for man through the shed blood of Calvary. Now we are seated in heavenly places with Christ Jesus. The essence of the position is to give us the privilege of ruling and making decrees with Him. Just as God rules, we rule. Just as Jesus decrees, we decree.

AUTHORITY AND DOMINION

The same way Jesus exercises authority and dominion is the same way we have been redeemed to exercise dominion and authority. Through the blood of Jesus and our redemptive transformation, God has positioned us as spiritual legislators. We are therefore the ones who truly rule and decree for things to come to pass.

God has given us this position to make the world to discover the power of dominion through this divine lift. When the Bible says that we are seated with Christ in heavenly places, it shows that God wants us to rule with Christ.

The truth is that, the Lord wants to use you to demonstrate how far He can go in His plan of redemption. Again, God wants to use you to bring His will to pass. Christ has no hands but your hands. He has no mouth with which to decree and enforce authority but your mouth. The Lord depends on you to prove to men and women that he is the only one who reigns without a rival.

PRAYER POINTS

1. Lord, give me the solution to any problem facing me, in the name of Jesus.

2. Trees of problems in my life, dry up to the roots, in the name of Jesus.

3. Walls of physical and spiritual opposition, fall after the order of Jericho, in the name of Jesus.

4. Let my king Uzziah die, so that I can see Your face, O Lord, in the name of Jesus.

5. I possess the power to pursue, overtake and recover my goods from spiritual Egyptians, in the name of Jesus.

6. Let every spell, jinxes and demonic incantations rendered against me be cancelled, in Jesus name.

7. I cancel every effect of any strange help, received from Egypt regarding this problem, in the name of Jesus.

8. Lord, heal all wounds and spiritual bullets sustained from attacks of the enemy, in the name of Jesus.

9. Let all hidden potentials and gifts that will make me great, stolen from me, be restored 21 fold, in the name of Jesus.

10. I. reject the spirit of regret, woes and disappointment, in the name of Jesus.

11. Lord, give me power for a new beginning, in the name of Jesus.

12. Lord, make my life a miracle and be glorified in every area of it, in the name of Jesus.

13. I command all demonic hindrances to my prosperity to be totally paralysed, in the name of Jesus.

14. Let every demonic bank, keeping my finances, be destroyed and release my finances, in the name of Jesus.

15. I bind every strongman, holding my finances captive, in the name of Jesus.

16. I possess all my possessions, in the name of Jesus.

17. Lord Jesus, I thank You for answering my prayer.

Chapter 8

The

Rulers

W e are to take charge, to rule over and take control. But unfortunately, the lives of many believers have remained a far cry from the ideal position which God earmarked for us. My heart is saddened, for the fact that many believers especially women are living in verted lives. While they are supposed to occupy positions of headship, they occupy very lowly positions. There is a lamentation in the scriptures which borders on the fact that, those for whom God has earmarked positions of prominence are displaying the characteristics of nonentities. This should not be so.

I have seen servants upon horses, and princes walking as servants upon the earth. Eccl. 10:7

AN ERROR

Herein lies the tragedy of modern day believers. We have mistakenly swapped positions. Therefore, we have allowed an error to characterise our lives. Folly is set in great dignity while the rich sit in low places.

Folly is set in great dignity, and the rich sit in low place. Eccl. 10:6

What are the consequences of this anomaly? Servants have taken over our horses and as princes and princesses we are trekking. This situation calls for an urgent remedy. It grieves the heart of God, to see princes and princesses occupying the lowly position of a servant while the ungodly who are supposed to serve us have stolen our horses.

The making of a prince or a princess is no small task. God has paid a great price to restore the dignity of man. Our redemption has caused God the precious blood of His beloved son, Jesus Christ. Having loved us and washed us in His blood, God has paid the greatest price in the history of the world. Why then should God make us princes and princesses only for us to live a beggarly live?

> *And hath made us kings and priests unto*
> *God and his Father; to him be glory and*
> *dominion for ever and ever. Amen.* Rev. 1:6.

A GREAT TRAGEDY

Why should a servant ride on a garnished horse while the soles of the feet of the price have developed blisters? This is a great tragedy. By the time a prince or a princess gets used to trekking, the thoughts of the fact that they have been set up to rule and issue decrees would have become a forgotten dream. It is unfortunate that we have gotten used to trekking. We have lost our staff of office. We have lost our sceptre of authority. Our mouths no longer issue decrees. We have left the place where we are supposed to issue commands. Rather than give orders, we have now allowed beggarly spirits to order us here and there.

Many who are supposed to cast out demons have become regular candidates on the deliverance ground. Many people who are supposed to exercise authority and dominion in the community are now battling with nightmares each night.

THE BURDEN

Oh that God will take us back to the days of our fathers. Oh that God will take us back to the days of Apostle J. A. Babalola, a man of God who was so anointed with powers that whenever he held a crusade or a revival, witches are not able to come anywhere around 30 kilometres from where he was ministering. Such satanic agents would have packed their bags and baggage and left the vicinity. They would only return when the man of God had left.

If you cannot enforce your fundamental gospel rights, how will you be able to tell witches and wizards to back off? As long as roles are swapped, you cannot exercise dominion. It is an anomaly, for servants to ride our horses. The horse is an instrument of glory and dignity. As far as vehicles were concerned in Bible days, the horse was a prominent means of transport. A horse was a symbol of class, royalty and position of prominence.

Princes were identified by the type of horses they rode. If you saw a man riding a horse, you would know that he is a prince. It was therefore a form of abnormality for a servant to ride resplendent upon horses. There is a lamentation going on in the heart of God. I want you to feel the pulse in the heart of the Almighty.

> *And she named the child Ichabod, saying, The glory is departed from Israel: because the ark of God was taken, and because of her father in law and her husband.* 1Sam. 4:21

> *And delivered his strength into captivity, and his glory into the enemy's hand.* Psa. 78:61

The crown is fallen from our head: woe unto us, that we have sinned! Lam. 5:16

He hath stripped me of my glory, and taken the crown from my head. Job 19:9

A LAMENTATION

When this happens, there is a problem. The moment the glory of man has been covered with shame, we know that destiny diverters are at work. Powers that tamper with destinies are having a field day. God's purpose has been derailed.

According to the scriptures, things have gone out of hand

They know not, neither will they understand; they walk on in darkness: all the foundations of the earth are out of course. Psa. 82:5

We live in ignorance. We walk blindfolded. We grope in palpable darkness. We have lost focus and there is no sense of direction. We have allowed the enemy to perpetuate terrible havoc. The result is that the entire world has now been converted to a casualty ward where there are lots of problems.

PRAYER POINTS

1. I break and loose myself, from every curse of financial poverty bondage, in the name of Jesus.

2. I release myself, from every conscious and unconscious covenant with the spirit of poverty, in the name of Jesus.

3. Let God arise and let every enemy of my financial breakthrough be scattered, in the name of Jesus.

4. O Lord, restore all my wasted years and efforts and convert them to blessings, in the name of Jesus.

5. Let the spirit of favour, be upon me everywhere I go concerning my finances, in the name of Jesus.

6. Father, I ask You, in the name of Jesus, to send ministering angels that bring in prosperity and funds into my finances.

7. Let men bless me anywhere I go, in Jesus' name.

8. I release my finances from the clutches of financial hunger, in the name of Jesus.

9. I loose angels, in the mighty name of Jesus, to go and create favour for my finances.

10. Let all financial hindrances be removed, in the name of Jesus.

11. I remove my name and those of my customers from the book of financial bankruptcy, in the name of Jesus.

12. Holy Spirit, be the senior partner in my finances, in the name of Jesus.

13. Every good thing, presently eluding my finances should flow into it, in the name of Jesus.

14. I reject, every spirit of financial embarrassment, in the name of Jesus.

15. Father, block every space causing unprofitable leakage to my finances, in the name of Jesus.

16. Let my finances become too hot to handle for dupes and demonic customers, in the name of Jesus.

17. Let spiritual magnetic power that attracts and keeps wealth be deposited in my finances, in the name of Jesus.

Chapter 9

Anointing
for
Accurate
PLACEMENT

Many lives have been turned upside down. Many lives have been rearranged by dark powers. Many destiny signposts have been lost. Life has lost meaning. The situation has gotten to a pandemic level. Many are going towards a wrong direction. This is extremely dangerous.

It is disheartening to see that, many lives are following the anti-clockwise direction. It is very dangerous when you are expected to be at the top and you are busy dozing off at the rear. Unfortunately, many have died without fulfilling the divine expectations for their life. Why don't you close your eyes and take this prayer point.

- *I shall not die without fulfilling God's agenda for my life, in the name of Jesus.*

You must pray until everything comes back to normal. There must be divine rearrangement. You must regain your position of headship. Enough of staying at the tail region. You must pray for divine restoration. You must ask God to catapult you from the tail region to the region of headship with immediate effect. Your mouth that has been busy begging around must be converted to a mouth that issues decrees.

73

CORRECT POSITIONING

The greatest good you can do to yourself is to work on correct positioning. You must get to a point where you are properly positioned, so that you will be able to issue appropriate decrees and exercise dominion over every work of darkness.

Nobody can remain at the valley and exercise dominion. A beggar cannot issue decrees. You cannot remain in the dungeon of life and rule. As long as you are handicapped socially or financially, you cannot come up with decrees which will be enforced. The first step you must take is to pray for divine reposition. No matter how talented you are, you cannot amount to anything if you remain at the tail region.

If you are the wisest man or woman in the community, you cannot command respect as long as you are backward. Being local champion will take you nowhere. You have to be a leader if you must command followership. You must be on top if you must issue decrees that will command attention globally.

THE PREPARATION

When God wants to prepare you to occupy a position whereby you will issue decrees, he has to first move you from the backward position and push you to the top where issuing decrees will be natural and easy. Whenever God begins to push you to the top, it is an indication of the fact that your season of decrees has come. When God decides to make you a man or a woman of authority, He will first make you uncomfortable with occupying the position of the tail. Inner dissatisfaction with the tail region and an inner desire to move up shows that God is preparing you for something great.

God does everything for a purpose. Every step taken by the Almighty has a purpose. For example, if God places a cup of water somewhere, there is a purpose for it. It is either He wants the water to become cold or He wants it to become slightly warm. Again, it is either He wants it to evaporate or congeal. Therefore, you must find out the purpose when God begins to prepare you ahead for something.

THE DIVINE PURPOSE

An understanding of the divine purpose will help you to maximise each opportunity and make use of your chances. You will be able to grab the opportunity and utilise it for your utmost good. When God created the world, He had a purpose for everything. There is a purpose for the stars and there is purpose for the moon. All of God's creation are created for a purpose. Nothing in your life happens by accident. God has a purpose or an agenda for your life.

God has not created you without a specific vacancy to occupy in His programme. God does not carry out useless exercises. He plans with wisdom and executes His plans with mathematical precision. God is meticulous as far as His plans and purposes are concerned.

Man is fearfully and wonderfully made. Your outlook, you stature and your general comportment is a pointer to what God wants to do with you. Your skills and your talent portrays the fact that God is up to something in your life. The place where you were born, the circumstances that surrounds your birth, your skills, your business acumen and your intelligence are indications of the fact that God has a unique agenda for your destiny. Nobody is by an accident. God made you for a unique reason.

I will praise thee; for I am fearfully and wonderfully made: marvellous are thy works; and that my soul knoweth right well. Psa. 139:14

It does not make any sense, for you to go about mournfully saying that you are a creature of circumstances. God made you wonderful and created you marvelously well. The skills you have acquired, the opportunities you have had and your hidden talents which God has deposited in your life is for a purpose.

God does not make mistakes, God designed you for a reason. You are never an after thought. Your creation is not a mistake. All that surrounds you show that God wants to achieve something with your life and your destiny.

PRAYER POINTS

1. I release my finances from the influences, control and domination of household wickedness, in the name of Jesus.

2. Let all satanic angels, deflecting blessings away from me, be completely paralysed, in the name of Jesus.

3. Let the evil effect of any strange money I have received or touched be neutralised, in the name of Jesus.

4. O Lord, teach me the divine secret of prosperity, in the name of Jesus.

5. Let the joy of the enemy over my financial life be converted to sorrow, in the name of Jesus.

6. Let all my blessings held captive locally or overseas be released to me, in the name of Jesus.

7. I bind, every anti-breakthrough, anti-miracle and anti-prosperity forces, in the name of Jesus.

8. Let my finances be too hot for any evil power to sit upon, in the name of Jesus.

9. O Lord, quicken my spirit to evolve money yielding ideas, in the name of Jesus. –

10. Let every spirit of debt and financial blockage be rendered impotent for my sake, in the name of Jesus.

11. O Lord, bring honey out of the rock for me and let me find the way where men say there is no way, in the name of Jesus.

12. Thank the Lord for answers to your prayers.

Chapter 10

The Mathematics *of* DESTINY

God is meticulously interested in you. He is the one who drew the lines on your palm. Your times are in His hands. The seasons of life which you have gone through are preparing you for something great. You are special in God's agenda.

You may wonder, How can I know my destiny? How can I come up with an understanding of what God wants me to do in life? What can I learn from my gifts and talents? What can I deduce from my strong points and unique endowments? Why am I who I am? Why am I where I am? These questions are pointers to your destiny.

THE POWER OF DESTINY

What is destiny? It is that which has already been concluded. Your destiny is God's agenda for your life that has already been decided. Your destiny is the rent for the life apportioned to you. Your destiny is why you are endowed with certain talents. Your destiny is the tithe you pay for your existence on earth.

You are not here by accident. You have an agenda to fulfil. You are not here on earth to go through life without making an impact. You have a particular thing to fulfil on earth. Your destiny is your portion. Your destiny is your role in the script of life. Your destiny is your contribution as you go through the pilgrimage of life.

UNDERSTANDING DESTINY

Your destiny is heaven's expectation for you. Your destiny is the track which you have been commanded to walk in. Your destiny is the portion of duty which God has assigned to you. Your destiny is your divinely appointed time. Your destiny is the sum total of the assignment which God will give you as you pass through this life.

Your destiny is your divinely ordained portion. It is that which God has commanded you to achieve. Your destiny is your duty, your task and your specific assignment. Your destiny is what you are expected to do to make this world a better place.

Your destiny is your relevance in life. Your destiny is what you are supposed to do in order to make your sphere of influence beneficial to your neighbours. Your destiny is the area where God wants to depend on you.

Destiny discovery is a task that must be done. You must pray your way to destiny fulfilment. You must begin with discovery, go ahead with execution and end up with fulfilment. Your destiny is your God-given dream. Your destiny is an idea that distinguishes you from the rest. It is what God shown you concerning your uniqueness.

DESTINY DEFINED

Being shown a symbol of your destiny is not enough. You must be able to unravel the mysteries behind your destiny. You must pray for divine analysis of the symbol of your destiny. For example if God shows you a vision where there is a pair of scissors you need to find out the meaning of the scissors. If God wants you to become a fashion designer, an artist or a fabric seller, you must find out. But if you rush into the vocation of a fashion designer when you are only meant to be a seller of modern fabrics, you will run into trouble in several areas.

Your destiny is something you must not miss. It is a vocation you cannot afford to neglect. If you are right on destiny, you will be right in every area of life. If you mess up with your destiny, you will mess up with every area of your life. Your destiny is crucial to your overall success in life. Your happiness in life depends on your destiny. Your usefulness to the society can only emanate from getting your destiny right. When your destiny receives a pass mark, your entire life will succeed.

Don't ever allow the devil to touch your destiny or tamper with the number purpose for which you are created by God. Your destiny is as important to you as the life which you live. Your destiny is as important to you as the air which you breathe.

PRAY!

I want you to pray with your hands laid on your chest.

- *My God, If I have been demonically rearranged, help me Lord and restore me, in the name of Jesus.*

If we fail to pray our destiny out of the dustbin of life, we may allow things to go from bad to worse. The devil is not interested in seeing you fulfil your destiny. The devil takes no delight in seeing you become who God wants you to become. The devil will rather sit down and watch everything concerning your destiny collapse. The devil will rather sit down and watch the total disintegration of your destiny. The only way you can make the devil happy is to dance to his tune by folding your hand while your destiny crumbles.

If you want the devil to laugh, just allow your destiny to be messed up significantly. If you want to issue a decree against the kingdom of darkness, they are ready to decree failure into your life and destiny. If you will not arise and make your captivity captive, the enemy will rush in and capture you.

PRAYER POINTS

1. O Lord, let every power challenging Your power in my life, be disgraced, in the name of Jesus.

2. Let every rage of the enemy be quenched, in the name of Jesus.

3. Let every evil imagination, fashioned against me be frustrated and disgraced, in the name of Jesus.

4. My glory, arise from the grave yard of backwardness, shine, in the name of Jesus.

5. Every arrow of confusion, be disgraced, in the name of Jesus.

6. Every assembly of affliction, scatter, in the name of Jesus.

7. Blood of Jesus, cause confusion in the blood bank of witchcraft, in the name of Jesus.

8. I decree against serpents and scorpions. Let their poison die, in the name of Jesus.

9. Night afflictions and oppressions, die, in the name of Jesus.

10. Every satanic trade-mark on my family, die, in the name of Jesus.

11. Every power struggling with the keys of my breakthroughs, die, in the name of Jesus.

12. I shall not become what my enemies want me to become, in the name of Jesus.

13. I shall excel, in every department of my life, in the name of Jesus.

14. O God, arise and roar like a terrible lion, and devour my portion, in the name of Jesus.

15. Vampire power, drinking the blood of my virtues, die, in the name of Jesus.

16. Every location assigned to dislocate my life, clear away, in the name of Jesus.

17. Every Goliath, boasting against my breakthroughs, die, in the name of Jesus.

18. My destiny, hear the word of the Lord, move to your next level, in the name of Jesus.

Chapter 11

The
Heavenly
EDICT

If God could open your eyes and see the amount of damage which the devil has done, you will not allow a single day to pass you by without issuing a decree. If you don't stop them, they will stop you. Therefore, you must stop them before they stop you. You must pursue the enemy or else they will pursue you. You must attack the kingdom of darkness or else they will attack you.

Take a look at the story below and you will discover that we must issue decrees as children of God if we do not want to become victims of attack from the kingdom of darkness.

> *And they came over unto the other side of the sea, into the country of the Gadarenes. And when he was come out of the ship, immediately there met him out of the tombs a man with an unclean spirit, Who had his dwelling among the tombs; and no man could bind him, no, not with chains: Because that he had been often bound with fetters and chains, and the chains had been plucked asunder by him, and the fetters broken in pieces: neither*

could any man tame him. And always, night and day, he was in the mountains, and in the tombs, crying, and cutting himself with stones. But when he saw Jesus afar off, he ran and worshipped him, And cried with a loud voice, and said, What have I to do with thee, Jesus, thou Son of the most high God? I adjure thee by God, that thou torment me not. For he said unto him, Come out of the man, thou unclean spirit. And he asked him, What is thy name? And he answered, saying, My name is Legion: for we are many. And he besought him much that he would not send them away out of the country. Now there was there nigh unto the mountains a great herd of swine feeding. And all the devils besought him, saying, Send us into the swine, that we may enter into them. And forthwith Jesus gave them leave. And the unclean spirits went out, and entered into the swine: and the herd ran violently down a steep place into the sea, (they were about two thousand;) and were choked in the sea.

And they that fed the swine fled, and told it in the city, and in the country. And they went out to see what it was that was done. And they come to Jesus, and see him that was possessed with the devil, and had the legion, sitting, and clothed, and in his right mind: and they were afraid. And they that saw it told them how it befell to him that was possessed with the devil, and also concerning the swine. And they began to pray him to depart out of their coasts. And when he was come into the ship, he that had been possessed with the devil prayed him that he might be with him. Howbeit Jesus suffered him not, but saith unto him, Go home to thy friends, and tell them how great things the Lord hath done for thee, and hath had compassion on thee. And he departed, and began to publish in Decapolis how great things Jesus had done for him: and all men did marvel. Mark 5:1-20

AN EVIL SPECIMEN

Here we are told a story concerning a man who became a specimen of the wickedness of demonic powers. The case of the man is pathetic. The Bible tells us that he came out of the tomb to meet Jesus. While others lived with their families the man in question was a companion of the dead.

While others preferred the companionship of normal human beings, the only thing that appealed to him was the eerie environment of the graveyard. No normal human being will want to live in a cemetery. But the man was so much out of his mind that he erected a tabernacle at the graveyard.

The graveyard is so far away from the place where human beings dwell. Most of the time, cemeteries are located in far places. It takes imagination to think of what goes on in the cemetery during the day and in the night. I am sure that you cannot even wish that your enemies should become tenants at the graveyard. The madness of the man in question had become so pronounced that the cemetery was the best atmosphere he desired.

While he lived at the cemetery, he was busy carrying out a mission of self destruction. Family members and friends must have given up on him. The most fortified chains, which had been used to bind him, broke like dry sticks. Nobody could make the man to tread the path of sanity. He had sleepless nights crying and cutting himself with stones. The case of the man had become so bad that he had become notorious and known as a mad man whose case has passed the highest mark of insanity.

A TERRIBLE ATTACK

What has happened to this man's destiny? While others were making progress in life, he was busy providing accommodation for thousands of demons. While his colleagues were playing host to important personalities in the society, he was busy playing host to thousand of demons. The demons had made him blind. They had made him insensitive. They had turned him to a one man riot; someone who would cut himself and at the same time be crying as a result of the pain.

How can anyone shed tears of pain and the same person continues to inflict pain on himself. Demons are terrible. Demons will order a witch to swallow her children and order the same witch to shed tears over the lost child. This is how wicked demonic spirits can be.

If you are not ready to fulfil your destiny, the devil is ready to unleash terror and wickedness upon you. The devil has no milk of human kindness. There is no pity in his dictionary.

DEAD DESTINIES

The Bible tells us;

> *Have respect unto the covenant: for the dark places of the earth are full of the habitations of cruelty.* Psa. 74:20

The tragedy of this generation is that many people's situation can be likened to the situation of the man described above. But unfortunately they demonstrate total ignorance concerning what they are going through. Many destinies are dead. Many destinies are stinking. Many destinies have been buried. Many destinies have been taken to the graveyard.

However, I have a good news for you. Just as the madman met Jesus out of the tomb, the Lord will meet you where you are at the moment. Even if the society have given up on you, the Lord will change your story and rearrange your destiny. Even if there are millions of demons tormenting you, they will jump out at the sound of the voice of the Master. God will decree a change in your situation and you will never be the same again.

Many lives have been rearrange and programmed to non achievement. Many lives have lost meaning. Many are trending a dangerous path where destiny has been completely swallowed up by evil powers.

Do you know that it is very dangerous to be alive without knowing your purpose for existence here on earth. It is very dangerous to live a purposeless life. When the enemy has tampered with your destiny, all you have is an empty shell. It is dangerous to keep moving towards the wrong direction. It is equally dangerous to be moving in an anticlockwise direction. It is dangerous to remain at the rear when you are supposed to be on top. Remaining below when God wants you to be on top is equally dangerous. Unfortunately, many have died without fulfilling their destinies.

PRAYER POINTS

1. I shall laugh my enemies to scorn, after the order of Elijah, in the name of Jesus.

2. This year, I shall sing my song and dance my dance, in the name of Jesus.

3. O God arise, and give me a turn around miracle, in the name of Jesus.

4. Do something in my life, O Lord, that will make me to celebrate, in the name of Jesus.

5. O God arise and open Your treasures unto me, in the name of Jesus.

6. O God arise and give me open heavens, in the name of Jesus.

7. O Lord, make me a candidate of supernatural surprises, in the name of Jesus.

8. By fire, by force, O God, launch me into my next level, in the name of Jesus.

9. O God arise and restore my past losses, in the name of Jesus.

10. Thou power of God, disgrace my detractors, in the name of Jesus.

11. Lord, contend with them that contend with me, in the name of Jesus.

12. Lord, let my generation celebrate me, in the name of Jesus.

13. Every arrow of mourning and sorrow, backfire, in the name of Jesus.

14. Lord, convert any pain in my life to gain, in the name of Jesus.

15. Give me my personal Pentecost. Give me fire to fight, O Lord, in the name of Jesus.

16. Lord, make me a blessing to my generations, in the name of Jesus.

17. I cancel tears, I cancel premature death, in the name of Jesus.

18. My Father, my Father, my Father, let people know I serve a living God, in the name of Jesus.

Chapter 12

The Simplicity of FAITH

This book will not be complete without an examination of the simplicity of faith. The power of a divine decree can not be put to use without faith. Faith is the energizer of those who issue divine decrees. A decree is a decree whether issued by a young officer or an aged officer. What is important is the status of the decree. While teaching on the power of faith, Jesus stated that all we need is faith that is the size of a mustard seed.

> *And Jesus said unto them, Because of your unbelief: for verily I say unto you, If ye have faith as a grain of mustard seed, ye shall say unto this mountain, Remove hence to yonder place; and it shall remove; and nothing shall be impossible unto you.* Matt. 17:20

GROWING FAITH

We often think that we need giant faith to move mountains. We do not really need an extraordinary faith, like the faith of great men of God before we can issue decrees against the kingdom of darkness. What the Bible describes is faith like a grain of mustard seed. If you have ever seen a grain of mustard before, you will understand what Jesus meant. The mustard seed is so tiny that the human breath will blow it away. This means that Jesus is saying that you can put to work your fledging faith. You can move your mountain. A little faith that is the size of a mustard seed will move it. You may be wondering, how can I make a decree when I am not a deliverance minister? How can I do exploits when I am not a super saint?

Jesus has simplified everything. Just a little faith is all you need. Let us learn a lesson from the way orders are given. A military officer who is not able to shout can give orders and be obeyed. The volume of his voice not withstanding, his command will be obeyed. In God's economy, when you give a command with a little faith, it will be obeyed. Beloved, you have faith. It takes faith to sit on the chair without worrying whether the chair will carry your weight. When you go to the super market to purchase a tin of milk or a can of juice, you simply pay and obtain the item. You may not open it for several days. This is an act of faith. Why will you believe that you were not sold a can of juice that is stuffed with sand. It is simply because you have faith. If we can apply faith, when we buy things at the grocery store, why can't we manifest faith in God?

JUST A LITTLE FAITH

The story below reveals the fact that just a little faith can give you results when you issue decrees

And when Jesus was passed over again by ship unto the other side, much people gathered unto him: and he was nigh unto the sea. And, behold, there cometh one of the rulers of the synagogue, Jairus by name; and when he saw him, he fell at his feet, And besought him greatly, saying, My little daughter lieth at the point of death: I pray thee, come and lay thy hands on her, that she may be healed; and she shall live. And Jesus went with him; and much people followed him, and thronged him. And a certain woman, which had an issue of blood twelve years, And had suffered many things of many physicians, and had spent all that she had, and was nothing bettered, but rather grew worse, When she had heard of Jesus, came in the press behind, and touched his garment. For she said, If I may touch but his clothes, I shall be whole. And straightway the fountain of her blood was dried up; and she felt in her body that she was healed of that plague. And Jesus, immediately knowing in himself that virtue had gone out of him, turned him about in the press, and said, Who touched my clothes? And his disciples said unto him, Thou seest the multitude thronging thee, and sayest thou, Who touched me? And he looked round about to see her that had done this thing. But the woman fearing and trembling, knowing what was done in her, came and fell down before him, and told him all the truth. And he said unto her, Daughter, thy faith hath made thee whole; go in peace, and be whole of thy plague. Mark 5:21-34

Here is the story of a woman who stole her miracle. She was not the primary object of the narrative. One of the rulers of the synagogue had sought the attention of Jesus on account of her daughter who was at the point of death. Jesus was in a hurry to attend to an urgent case.

One woman was in the crowd. There was nothing unusual about her. She had no political leader to help her book an appointment with Jesus. She was not sure that if she shouted she would secure the attention of Jesus. She was no spiritual giant. But she had a little faith like a grain of mustard seed. She believed that she could touch the garment of Jesus and be free from her nagging haemorrhage.

She made a fast move and touched the helm of the garment of Jesus. Hardly had she made the move than she experienced instantaneous healing. The flow of blood stopped and she felt healing in her body. The people around Jesus were too busy to take note of what had happened. There was no casting out of devils. There was no anointing with oil. It was just a simple miracle brought about by a simple touch. Interestingly, only two people knew that a miracle had taken place, the healer and the healed.

> *And straightway the fountain of her blood was dried up; and she felt in her body that she was healed of that plague. And Jesus, immediately knowing in himself that*

103

> *virtue had gone out of him, turned him*
> *about in the press, and said, Who touched*
> *my clothes?* Mark 5:29-30

Jesus knew that someone had received a miracle. He knew that healing virtue had gone out of him.

> *And his disciples said unto him, Thou*
> *seest the multitude thronging thee, and*
> *sayest thou, Who touched me?* Mark 5:31

The disciples could not understand how an innocent touch by a sick woman could have drawn virtue from the body of Jesus. By the time the woman came out, it became clear that she had gotten her healing by manifesting a simple faith.

> *And he said unto her, Daughter, thy faith*
> *hath made thee whole; go in peace, and*
> *be whole of thy plague.* Mark 5:34

What do we learn here? If a sick woman could manifest faith, why can't you manifest the same level of faith?

The woman touched the garment of Jesus, as an act of faith. Jesus zeroed in on the woman's faith when he said, *"thy faith had made thee whole."*

SIMPLE FAITH

Having gotten so far in this book, all you need to issue decrees is simple faith. You do not need to attend a Bible school before you can become a decree issuing believer. Just open your mouth and the word of faith will come out powerfully. Again, the Bible says!

> *But the righteousness which is of faith speaketh on this wise, Say not in thine heart, Who shall ascend into heaven? (that is, to bring Christ down from above.) Or, Who shall descend into the deep? (that is, to bring up Christ again from the dead.) But what saith it? The word is nigh thee, even in thy mouth, and in thy heart: that is, the word of faith, which we preach; That if thou shalt confess with thy mouth the Lord Jesus, and shalt believe in thine heart that God hath raised him from the dead, thou shalt*

be saved. For with the heart man believeth unto righteousness; and with the mouth confession is made unto salvation. For the scripture saith, Whosoever believeth on him shall not be ashamed. Rom. 10:6-11

The word of faith is simple. The decree of faith is easy. Just say it and it shall come to pass. Decree an uncommon change today and God shall bring it to pass. God will enforce every decree which you shall issue. Amen.

PRAYER POINTS

1. This year, I must not fail, in the name of Jesus.

2. My Father, deliver me from strange battles, in the name of Jesus.

3. My Father, cause this year to be my year of jubilee and rejoicing, in the name of Jesus.

4. O God arise and fill my mouth with laughter, in the name of Jesus.

5. O God arise and let my tears expire, in the name of Jesus.

6. O God arise and let my shame expire, in the name of Jesus.

7. I receive an uncommon wisdom to excel, in the name of Jesus.

8. My Father, accelerate my speed and close the gap between where I am and where I should be in life, in the name of Jesus.

9. Every power assigned to put off my light, receive confusion, in the name of Jesus.

10. Let the rainbow of glory appear in my situation, in the name of Jesus.

11. Conspiracy against my life, lift away into the sea, in the name of Jesus.

12. Captivity, arise, trouble my captivity, in the name of Jesus.

13. I recover, all my known and unknown opportunities, in the name of Jesus.

14. I put on my dancing shoes, my sorrows are over, in the name of Jesus.

15. Open Your abundance unto me, O Lord, in the name of Jesus.

16. Sword of God, cast off every satanic attachment from my life, in the name of Jesus.

17. Darkness, break away from my life, in the name of Jesus.

18. Any mouth cursing me, be eaten by poison, in the name of Jesus.

Chapter 13

Moving
to the
Other Side

M any of us are so familiar with God's word that we often take it for granted. We mistakenly equate the words of men with the words of the Ancient of Days. Therefore, the changes which we desire, are nowhere to be found. If you think deeply at this moment, you will remember that God has given you a lot of promises. Some of these promises have been forgotten while a good number have been taken for grated. This situation is universal. It is simply because words have lost value with us. Many people around us play with words. Some people simply forget the words they speak as soon as they utter them. As far as God is concerned, it is a different situation. God honours His words. God stands by His words to perform it.

Then said the LORD unto me, Thou hast well seen: for I will hasten my word to perform it. Jer. 1:12

IT IS SETTLED

God never jokes with His words. When he speaks, it is settled. He declares what must surely come to pass. What we need to do is to learn how to hold on to the word of God, the moment it is spoken. Now that you know what a decree is all about, you need to know that God's word when spoken has the status of a decree. The moment the Almighty speaks, you are sure there shall be a performance

> *And blessed is she that believed: for there shall be a performance of those things which were told her from the Lord.* Luke 1:45

All you need to do is to believe that certainly there shall be a performance of what God has spoken. Let us go through the scriptures and meditate on certain instances when divine pronouncements were made and they were fulfilled to the letter.

> *And the same day, when the even was come, he saith unto them, Let us pass over unto the other side.* Mark 4:35

Here, Jesus told the disciples "Let us pass over to the other side". They heard the words of Jesus but they soon forgot the divine instruction when trouble came up.

And there arose a great storm of wind, and the waves beat into the ship, so that it was now full. And he was in the hinder part of the ship, asleep on a pillow: and they awake him, and say unto him, Master, carest thou not that we perish?
Mark 4:37-38

THE OTHER SIDE

According to the words of Jesus, the destination was the other side. But, the disciples were so fearful that they asked "Master carest not that we perish!" The Lord had pronounced that they would get to the other side. But the storms made them to entertain the fear of perishing in the sea. Beloved, if God says you are getting to the other side; you are already there as far as He is concerned. Nothing will happen to you between where you are and the other side where the Lord has prophetically positioned you.

Storms may rage, problems may come up, satanic volcanoes may erupt, and enemies may try to distract you, nobody can change the verdict of the Almighty. What God says concerning you will come to pass.

Whatever the enemy says will be rendered null and void. The voice of God will remain true. The voice of the enemy will soon be silenced.

> *But ye are forgers of lies, ye are all physicians of no value. O that ye would altogether hold your peace! and it should be your wisdom.* Job 13:4-5

The storm was orchestrated by the enemy. It brought up a contest between the word of the Lord, and the word of the enemy. But the Bible says,

> *There are many devices in a man's heart; nevertheless the counsel of the LORD, that shall stand.* Prov. 19:21

Unfortunately, the disciples chose to echo the counsel of the enemy by asking whether the Lord cared if they perish. They were with the Master of oceans and sea. How could they perish when they were blessed with the presence of the One who created the sea and the wind? At least, they would have known that the most violent storm in the world is left with no other option than to obey the King of kings and the Lord of lords. We can learn a lesson from what Jesus did. He simply spoke the word and rested his head peacefully on a pillow, He had declared that the disciples would pass over to the other side.

The beauty of the incident is that Jesus spoke to the wind and there was calm. There is a lesson you can learn from the manner with which Jesus addressed the wind and brought a great calm into sea. God is a God of purpose. Everything He does shows that He has an end in view. When the storm came up, there was a purpose. When the Lord ordered it to stop, there was a purpose also. Everything was done in order to bring the word of God to pass.

> *And they came over unto the other side of the sea, into the country of the Gadarenes.* Mark 5:1

Whatever happens, all the events around you will be divinely guided to accomplish one thing - fulfilling what God has spoken. Two unforgettable phrases should be noted

1. Let us pass over to the other side
2. And they came over to the other side.

114

THE DECREE

The decree of the Almighty is that the disciples would pass over to the other side. But, the enemy tried to come up with a pseudo decree saying that the disciples would not get to the other side. Unknown to the power of the enemy, God's word has been settled. Nobody can challenge the Almighty. The storm was not strong enough to prevent them from getting to their prophetic destination. In the same vein, no power can prevent you from getting to your place of destiny.

Once God has spoken, it shall come to pass. Do not allow the enemy to intimidate you. Do not allow the enemy to put you under, when God has destined you for the top. You are destined for the other side where there is victory, blessings, promotion, and mighty signs and wonders. Nothing on earth can prevent you from ascending your throne. You are a child of destiny. Your heavenly Father has spoken good concerning you. And it shall come to pass. Every promise, every prophetic declaration and the totality of the agenda of heaven, shall all come to pass. No storm from the kingdom of darkness shall prevent you from getting to your destination.

115

God has surveyed the length and the breadth of the territories you will occupy. You will get there. Storms are temporary. But, what God has spoken is permanent. The power of God will swallow every storm sponsored by the devil. The enemy will want to disgrace you, but you shall prevail. By the time God has fulfilled His agenda, you are the one who will disgrace the enemy. You will get to the top. You will make it. You shall celebrate outstanding success. You shall be celebrated. Just as the disciples got to the other side, you shall get to the other side too. Your testimony shall be outstanding . Your story shall attract international attention, in the name of Jesus.

PRAYER POINTS

1. I decree by fire and thunder, that I shall not die before the manifestation of my miracles, in the name of Jesus.

2. Oh God, arise and hear me in the day of trouble, in the name of Jesus.

3. Oh Lord, I run into Your name that is a strong tower, in the name of Jesus.

4. Oh Lord, let all my stubborn problems be buried, in the name of Jesus.

5. I shall not die because of my problems, in the name of Jesus.

6. I shall not be disgraced because of my problems, in the name of Jesus.

7. Let the fire of God, begin to attack all miracle hijackers assigned against my life, in the name of Jesus.

8. God has made me a product of His possibility, no good thing shall be impossible for me, in the name of Jesus.

117

9. Every curse and covenant of impossibility over my life, break, in the name of Jesus.

10. Thou Goliath of impossibility in my life, die, in the name of Jesus.

11. I shall not die undiscovered, in the name of Jesus.

12. I shall not die unused and unsung, in the name of Jesus.

13. I shall not die uncelebrated and unmissed, in the name of Jesus.

14. I shall not die unfruitful and unfulfilled, in the name of Jesus.

15. Every good thing, the enemy has swallowed in my life, be vomited, in the name of Jesus.

16. Oh God arise, and send me help from the sanctuary and strengthen me out of Zion, in the name of Jesus.

17. Let my rescue and deliverance be announced from heaven, in the name of Jesus.

Chapter 14

You will
get

THERE

Y ou will get to the other side where God shall open a new page in the history of your life. The God of heaven and earth who has spoken good concerning you, will give you pleasant surprises. He will launch you into the realm of signs and wonders. He will catapult you to greatness. He will comfort you on every side and increase your greatness. Your testimony shall give birth to countless number of testimonies. Beloved, hold on to your God-given dreams. You will make it. No power shall turn your joy to sorrow. God shall watch over His word concerning your life to perform it. Welcome to your season of greatness.

So far, we have seen what it takes for God to speak a word concerning you and fulfil it. Now, we shall see what it takes for God to speak a word to councel the agenda of darkness. We shall draw certain lessons from the incident below.

> *And on the morrow, when they were come from Bethany, he was hungry: And seeing a fig tree afar off having leaves, he came, if haply he might find any thing thereon: and when he came to it, he found nothing but leaves; for the time of figs*

> *was not yet. And Jesus answered and*
> *said unto it, No man eat fruit of thee*
> *hereafter for ever. And his disciples*
> *heard it.* Mark 11:12-4

This is a classical example of the mystery of verbal warfare. It is a simple story but we can draw lessons on spiritual warfare from it. Jesus had an encounter with a fruitless fig tree. It was a tree with nothing but leaves. Jesus wanted the disciples to know that certain things can be cursed. Jesus simply said *"No man eat fruit of thee hereafter for ever"* and that was it. From the moment Jesus spoke, the deed had been done. But the tree was still standing on the same spot. The mystery of verbal warfare is that immediately Jesus spoke, the tree died. The disciples did not see any sign of death, they would have wondered why the tree still flaunted green leaves. They soon learnt a great lesson.

> *And in the morning, as they passed by,*
> *they saw the fig tree dried up from the*
> *roots. And Peter calling to remembrance*
> *saith unto him, Master, behold, the fig*
> *tree which thou cursedst is withered*
> *away.* Mark 11:20-21

121

AMAZING !

The disciples expressed shock and surprise when they discovered that by the next day, the fig tree had dried from the roots. It was Peter who remembered that Jesus had cursed the fig tree the previous day. The disciples all became excited. But Jesus was not moved as He knew that the tree was dead the moment He pronounced a curse upon it. Jesus, therefore, taught the disciples a great lesson on faith.

> *And Jesus answering saith unto them, Have faith in God. For verily I say unto you, That whosoever shall say unto this mountain, Be thou removed, and be thou cast into the sea; and shall not doubt in his heart, but shall believe that those things which he saith shall come to pass; he shall have whatsoever he saith. Therefore I say unto you, What things soever ye desire, when ye pray, believe that ye receive them, and ye shall have them.* Mark 11:22-24

SPIRITUAL WARFARE

There is a lesson we must learn in the area of spiritual warfare. As you pray you must manifest corresponding faith, as soon as you issue a decree. Heaven enforces your decree immediately you pronounce it. The tree may be standing as if nothing had happened at that moment, but the truth is that it is gone. Jesus merely decreed that the tree would be fruitless for life. But, the power of the decree of the Lord caused the tree to wither from its roots. Beloved, I do not know what the enemy is doing in order to attack you. But, one thing I know is that just one decree from the throne of heaven will make the tree of darkness to dry from its roots. Remember the words of Jesus.

> *But he answered and said, Every plant, which my heavenly Father hath not planted, shall be rooted up.* Matt. 15:13

There is an eternal decree and it is this *"Whatever God has not planted shall be uprooted."* The enemy can go ahead and plant anything, but the decree of heaven is this. *"It shall be rooted up."* The plantation of sickness and infirmities shall be rooted up. The plantations of marital failure shall be rooted up. The plantations of failure and poverty shall be rooted up. The decree of the God who answers by fire shall locate the roots of evil plantation and all the plantations shall wither in the mighty name of Jesus. How will this happen? The Bible has given us a secret. Whatever the enemy is doing to hinder your destiny, shall scatter unto desolation. The decree of the Almighty will nullify every decree of darkness. You will come up with an outstanding testimony.

PRAYER POINTS

1. Before I finished praying these prayers, Oh Lord, let Your angels move into action on my behalf, in the name of Jesus.

2. Every Prince of Persia and all territorial spirits around me, that are hindering the manifestation of God's miracle in my life, scatter, in the name of Jesus.

3. I bind and cast out of my vicinity, all prayer and miracle blockers, in the name of Jesus.

4. You miracle hijackers, release my miracles now by fire, in the name of Jesus.

5. Every satanic umbrella, preventing the heavenly showers of blessings from falling on me, catch fire, in the name of Jesus.

6. Oh God, arise and let my heavens open right now, in the name of Jesus.

7. I shall not give up, because I have believed to see the goodness of the Lord in the land of the living, in the name of Jesus.

8. O Lord, let my soul be prevented from death, my eyes from tears and my feet from falling, in the name of Jesus.

9. People will hear my testimonies and glorify the name of God in my life, in the name of Jesus.

10. My Father, let Your divine intervention in my life bring souls to the kingdom of God, in the name of Jesus.

11. I use the blood of Jesus to fight and defeat every spirit of impossibility in my life, in the name of Jesus.

12. I release myself from the collective captivity of impossibility, in the name of Jesus.

13. Every seed, root and tentacles of impossibility in my life, die, in the name of Jesus.

14. I withdraw my name and all about my life, from the altar of impossibility, in the name of Jesus.

15. I refuse to swim in the oceans of impossibility, in the name of Jesus.

Chapter 15

Prayer
DECREES

DAY ONE

I DECREE BREAKTHROUGH

1. Let all contrary spiritual handwriting against me, be blotted out by the power in the blood of Jesus.

2. Thou Rock of Ages, fall upon and scatter all the powers of the strongman, assigned against me, in the name of Jesus.

3. Let every curse of the enemy, be turned to blessings for me, in the name of Jesus.

4. Let all evil weapons of the enemy, assigned against my life be cut into pieces, in the name of Jesus.

5. Let the excellency of dignity and power, make me excel, in the name of Jesus.

6. Storms of failure, poverty and lack of development in my life, die, in the name of Jesus.

7. Evil prophecies of familiar spirits and hosts of darkness, against my life, die, in the name of Jesus.

8. Every contrary fire, set against my life, be quenched, in the name of Jesus.

9. Every good door shut against my life, be opened by fire, in the name of Jesus.

10. Let the wall of protection of my enemies, fall upon them, in the name of Jesus.

11. Every evil visitor, assigned against my life, fall down and die, in the name of Jesus.

12. Every power assigned to hinder my star from shining, fall down and die, in the name of Jesus.

13. Every evil work against the star of my life, die, in the name of Jesus.

14. Let the alliance of my enemies receive confusion, in the name of Jesus.

15. Let every valley of death and suffering, assigned against my life turn to blessings for me, in the name of Jesus.

16. I receive freedom in all areas of life, in the name of Jesus.

17. Any contrary handwriting against me in heaven, on earth or underneath the earth, be blotted out by the power in the blood of Jesus.

18. All satanic lions, roaring to swallow up my star, die, in the name of Jesus.

19. Every evil stronghold, behind the problems in my life, be pulled down, in the name of Jesus.

20. Let the salvation of God visit my life and set me up, in the name of Jesus.

21. Every spiritual storm of poverty, be silenced, in the name of Jesus.

22. Let all my enemies be as chaff before the wind; and let the angels of the Lord chase them, in the name of Jesus.

23. Every evil seed growing in my life, be uprooted by fire, in the name of Jesus.

24. Let the blood of Jesus roll every Egyptian reproach away from my life, in the name of Jesus.

25. Let them be afraid and brought to confusion all who rejoice at my downfall, in the name of Jesus.

26. Let my enemies be clothed with shame and disgrace, in the name of Jesus.

27. Let the ways of the enemy be darkened and slippery, and the angles of the Lord persecute them, in the name of Jesus.

28. Let destruction come upon my enemy unawares: and let his net that he had hid catch himself, into that very destruction let him fall, in the name of Jesus.

29. Let all the spiritual links, that connect me with the spirit world be broken, in the name of Jesus.

30. My star shall rise to fall no more, in the name of Jesus.

31. Begin to thank God for answering your prayers

DAY TWO

I DECREE AN UNCOMMON CHANGE

1. Lord, let Jesus increase in my heart and in all that is associated with my life, in the name of Jesus.

2. Let God's scepter of righteousness be witnessed and experienced in my life, in the name of Jesus.

3. O Lord, take Your place in my life, in my family and in all departments of my life, in Jesus' name.

4. O Lord, wake me up from deep and spiritual slumber, in the name of Jesus.

5. O Lord, renew my mind, in the name of Jesus.

6. Let the command of the Lord bring light to my eyes and revival to my soul, in the name of Jesus.

7. Lord Jesus, walk on my waters, in the name of Jesus.

8. O Lord, deliver me and my family from the spirit of fear and inconsistency, in the name of Jesus.

9. Let the angels of God roll back, every stone of limitation and bondage in my family, in the name of Jesus.

10. Let the resurrection power that raised Christ from the dead overthrow spiritual entities that are sitting on the gates of my life, in the name of Jesus.

11. Let the mountains of oppression, ignorance and idolatry be uprooted from my family line, in the name of Jesus.

12. Let the light of Jesus expose every darkness and every den of wickedness in my family. Let them be replaced with the light of Your countenance, O Lord, in the name of Jesus.

13. Let the light of God drown the walls of darkness around my life, in the name of Jesus.

14. Let the dayspring take the earth by the edges and shake out all the wicked structures in my life, in the name of Jesus.

15. O God, arise and shake all the foundations of idolatry, witchcraft out of my life, in Jesus' name.

16. Let the morning star of Christ and the brightness of His presence consume every iota of darkness and satanic strongholds around my house, in the name of Jesus.

17. Lord, by a strong east wind, drive away all the darkness that has surrounded my life all this while, in the name of Jesus.

18. Let the dayspring shake the foundations of all satanic structures around my life, in Jesus' name.

19. Let the earth vomit the wicked and silence the proud, in the name of Jesus.

20. O Lord, throw into confusion, all the chariots of hell, all the distractions, and the spirit of deception that seeks to derail the progress of my life, in the name of Jesus.

21. O Lord, grant me refuge and rest, under Your wings, in the name of Jesus.

22. O Lord, deliver me from every terror of the night and every arrow that flies by day, in Jesus' name.

23. O Lord, do a rearrangement in my life and ministry, in the name of Jesus.

24. O God, illuminate my horizon, in Jesus' name.

25. Let the protection of the Lord become the portion of my household, in the name of Jesus.

26. Let the rays of the powerful light of God introduce new ideas, new perceptions, new ways and methods of doing things after the order of the word of God into my life, in the name of Jesus.

27. Let the Lord protect and gladden my heart, in the name of Jesus.

28. Let the Lord overthrow the stronghold of my enemies and be overthrown without mercy, in the name of Jesus.

29. Let my healing come quickly like the dawn and my path shine even brighter than the full light of day, in the name of Jesus.

30. Let God arise and let Him scatter and disband all the wicked spirits from my land, in the name of Jesus.

31. I activate the benefits of the blood of Jesus over my life, and my household, in the name of Jesus.

32. O Lord, anoint my head with Your oil, bless my water and bread to eat of the fat of this land, in the name of Jesus.

DAY THREE

I DECREE UNCOMMON BLESSINGS

1. Thank the Lord from the bottom of your heart for what He will use this prayer programme to do in your life.

2. I reject, every backward journey, in the name of Jesus.

3. I paralyse, every strongman assigned to this institution, in the name of Jesus.

4. Let every agent of shame, working against me, be paralysed, in the name of Jesus.

5. I paralyse the activities of household wickedness over my life, in the name of Jesus.

6. I quench, every strange fire, emanating from evil tongues against me, in the name of Jesus.

7. Lord, give me power for maximum achievement in this place, in the name of Jesus.

8. O Lord, give me the confronting authority to achieve effortless results, in the name of Jesus.

9. Lord, fill me with wisdom like an angel, in Jesus' name.

10. I break, every curse of fruitlessness placed upon my life, in the name of Jesus.

11. I break, every curse of untimely death, in the name of Jesus.

12. Lord, fortify me with Your power, in the name of Jesus.

13. Let the counter-movement of the Holy Spirit frustrate every evil vice against me, in the name of Jesus.

14. Father Lord, give me the tongue of the learned, in the name of Jesus.

15. Lord, make my voice the voice of peace, deliverance and power, in the name of Jesus.

16. Lord, give me divine direction that will propel this institution to greatness through me, in the name of Jesus.

17. Every power, assigned to use my family, job, etc to torment me, be paralysed, in the name of Jesus.

18. Lord Jesus, give me an excellence spirit, in the name of Jesus.

19. Thank God for answered prayers.

20. Thank the Lord because He alone can let you advance.

21. O Lord, bring me into favour with all those who will decide on my employment

22. O Lord, cause a divine substitution to happen if this is what will move me ahead, in the name of Jesus.

23. I reject the spirit of the tail and I claim the spirit of the head, in the name of Jesus.

24. I command all evil records planted by the devil in anyone's mind against my employment to be shattered to pieces, in the name of Jesus.

25. O Lord, transfer, remove or change all human agents that are bent on stopping my employment, in the name of Jesus.

26. I receive the anointing to excel above my contemporaries, in the name of Jesus.

27. Lord, catapult me into greatness as You did for Daniel in the land of Babylon, in the name of Jesus.

28. I bind, every strongman delegated to hinder my progress, in the name of Jesus.

29. O Lord, dispatch Your angels to roll away every stumbling block to my employment, in the name of Jesus.

30. I bind and render to naught the spirit of . . . . *(pick from the under listed)*, in the mighty name of Jesus.
    - demonic antagonism   - strife
    - unprofitable questions   - confusion
    - marginal success   - mind blankness
    - wrong words   - mind dullness
    - bad feet/bad luck   - memory failure
    - demonic opinions against me
    - unprofitable controversies
    - evil collaborators   - demonic logic
    - unprofitable interviews

31. I claim the position of . . . . . . , in the mighty name of Jesus *(name the specific position being sought)*.

32. Lord, hammer my matter into the mind of those who will assist me so that they do not suffer from a demonic loss of memory, in the name of Jesus.

33. I paralyse the handiwork of house hold enemies and envious agents, in this matter, in the name of Jesus.

34. Let all adversaries of my breakthroughs be put to shame, in the name of Jesus.

35. I claim the power to overcome and to excel amongst all competitors, in the name of Jesus.

36. Let any decision by any panel be favourable unto me, in the name of Jesus.

37. All competitors with me in this issue will find my defeat unattainable, in the name of Jesus.

38. Praise the Lord for answered prayers.

39. Holy Spirit, multiply Your grace upon my life, in the name of Jesus.

40. Anointing of revelation, fall upon my spirit man, in the name of Jesus.

41. Anointing of wisdom, fall upon my inner man, in the name of Jesus.

42. Holy Ghost Fire, open the eyes of my spirit, in the name of Jesus.

43. Oh Lord, let all the angels assigned to assist me in my ministry, receive fire, in the name of Jesus.

44. Any power that has arrested my angels, be arrested and let my angels be released, in the name of Jesus.

45. Oh Mighty hand of God, fall upon me for ministry and protection, in the name of Jesus.

46. Oh Lord, let me and my descendants dwell under the shadow of the Almighty all the days of our lives, in the name of Jesus.

47. Oh Lord, keep me, my ministry, my family and my descendants after me in Your pavilion, in the name of Jesus. - for in Your pavilion, evil arrows cannot locate me.

48. Evil arrows that came into my life by night, jump out and come out of my life by night, in the name of Jesus.

49. Oh Lord God of Elijah, arise in Your power and let all my enemies fall before me, in the name of Jesus.

50. Oh Lord, whenever my enemies plan any attack against me in the future, let their counsel fall into foolishness, in the name of Jesus.

51. Oh Lord, whenever my enemies takes evil decision against me, let Your truth deliver according to Thy Word, in the name of Jesus. *(pray for those who are victims of false accusations and slander from brethren in the house of God)*.

52. Oh Lord, Man of War, destroy the teeth of all those the devil will use against me in Your sanctuary, in the name of Jesus.

53. Oh Lord, break me, and mould me for Your glory, in the name of Jesus.

54. Every synagogue of Satan, erected against me, fall down before me now, for I am the beloved of the Lord, in the name of Jesus.

55. Anything in me, that will allow the arrow of the enemy to prosper, be removed now, in the name of Jesus.

56. Every demonic alteration of my destiny, lose your hold upon my life and come out of my foundation, in the name of Jesus.

57. All the powers behind demonic alteration of my destiny, die, in the name of Jesus.

58. Any power, behind demonic alteration of my handwriting and virtues, die, in the name of Jesus.

59. Demonic marriage, lose your hold over my life and be purged out of my foundation, in the name of Jesus.

60. Every strange child, assigned to me in the dream, be roasted by fire, in the name of Jesus.

61. I command the fire of God to pursue all strange children and women assigned to me in the dream, in the name of Jesus.

62. Every evil laying on of hands, loose your hold over my life and be purged out of my foundation, in the name of Jesus.

63. Evil idols from my father's house, fight against idols form my mothers house and destroy yourselves, in the name of Jesus.

64. Every idol in my place of birth, holding down my destiny, be roasted by fire, in the name of Jesus.

65. Every demonic authority, attacking my life as a result of my past relationship with strange sexual partners, be roasted by fire, in the name of Jesus.

66. Every demon activated against me, go back to your owner, in the name of Jesus.

67. All demon and principalities, assigned against me, be decommissioned, in the name of Jesus.

68. Failure shall not slaughter my destiny, in the name of Jesus.

69. I have come to Zion, my destiny must change, in the name of Jesus.

70. O Lord, take away my destiny from the hands of men, in the name of Jesus.

71. Satan, you will not settle down on my destiny, in the name of Jesus.

72. My destiny shall not suffer affliction, in the name of Jesus.

73. Today, I raise up the altar of continuous prosperity upon my destiny, in the name of Jesus.

74. The enemy will not convert my destiny to rags, in the name of Jesus.

75. Oh Lord, give me new eyes to see into my destiny, in the name of Jesus.

76. The mouth of the wicked shall not speak again against my destiny, in the name of Jesus.

77. Let the spirit of excellence come upon me, in the name of Jesus.

78. The rod of the wicked shall not rest upon my life, in the name of Jesus.

79. I enter into my prophetic destiny, in the name of Jesus.

80. The leaf of my destiny shall not wither, in the name of Jesus.

81. The powers that move people out of Gods destiny shall not locate me, in the name of Jesus.

82. My destiny, reject poverty, in the name of Jesus.

83. I forbid evil hands to perform their enterprise upon my destiny, in the name of Jesus.

84. Any evil hand, that will point against my destiny this year shall dry up, in the name of Jesus.

85. Every switch designed to put on the light of my destiny, operate by fire, in the name of Jesus.

86. I reject, every satanic alternative for my destiny, in the name of Jesus.

87. Evil caldrons, you will not cook up my destiny, in the name of Jesus.

88. Destiny swallowers, vomit my destiny, in the name of Jesus.

89. I recover my stolen vehicle of destiny, in the name of Jesus.

90. O Lord, anoint my destiny afresh, in the name of Jesus.

91. I overthrow, every satanic re-arrangement programmed against my destiny, in Jesus' name.

92. I refuse to miss my destiny in life, in the name of Jesus.

93. I refuse to accept satanic substitute for my destiny, in the name of Jesus.

94. I revoke every ownership on my destiny, in the name of Jesus.

95. I set judgement against every evil altar, erected against my destiny, in the name of Jesus.

96. I reject every satanic rearrangement of my destiny, in the name of Jesus.

97. I paralyse every destiny polluter, in the name of Jesus.

98. I reject and renounce destiny-demoting names and I nullify their evil effects upon my destiny, in the name of Jesus.

99. I refuse to operate below my divine destiny, in the name of Jesus.

100. I command all powers of darkness assigned to my destiny to leave and never to return, in the name of Jesus.

101. Conspiracy of darkness against my destiny, scatter by fire, in the name of Jesus.

102. Whether Satan likes it or not, I wake to my destiny by fire, in the name of Jesus.

103. The fire of the enemy against my destiny shall backfire, in the name of Jesus.

104. No weapon formed against my destiny shall prosper, in the name of Jesus.

105. I reject, every rearrangement of my destiny by household wickedness, in the name of Jesus.

106. I paralyse, every satanic opportunity contending against my life, in the name of Jesus.

107. I dismantle, spiritual devices working against my destiny, in the name of Jesus.

108. I take authority over every witchcraft prayer working against my destiny, in the name of Jesus.

109. I am a hot coal of fire, any herbalist that tampers with my destiny gets burnt, in the name of Jesus.

110. I reject and renounce destiny-demoting devices, in the name of Jesus.

111. I silence every oracle speaking against my destiny, in the name of Jesus.

112. I destroy the gates of violent spirits that are working against my destiny, in the name of Jesus.

113. I scatter every sacrifice made against my destiny, in the name of Jesus.

114. Any satanic statement programmed into the sun, moon and stars against my destiny, I revoke you by fire, in the name of Jesus.

115. This month, you must cooperate with my destiny, in the name of Jesus.

116. I overturn and destroy any wicked pattern of dream pollution attached to my destiny, in the name of Jesus.

117. I render all evil attacks against my potential and destiny impotent, in the name of Jesus.

118. Praise the Lord for answered prayers.

191. When The Deliverer Need Deliverance
192. When The Enemy Hides
193. When Things Get Hard
194. When You Are Knocked Down
195. When You Are Under Attack
196. When You Need A Change
197. Where Is Your Faith?
198. While Men Slept
199. Woman! Thou Art Loosed.
200. Your Battle And Your Strategy
201. Your Foundation And Destiny
202. Your Mouth And Your Deliverance
203. Your Mouth And Your Warfare

YORUBA PUBLICATIONS

1. Adura Agbayori
2. Adura ti Nsi Oke Ni'di
3. Ojo Adura

FRENCH PUBLICATIONS

1. Pluie De Priere
2. Espirit De Vagabondage
3. En Finir Avec Les Forces Malefiques De La Maison De Ton Pere
4. Que I'envoutement Perisse
5. Frappez I'adversaire Et Il Fuira

31. Pouvoir Contre Les Demond Tropicaux
32. Le Programme De Tranfert De Richesse
33. Les Etudiants A l'ecole De La Peur
34. L'etoile Dans Votre Ciel
35. Les Saisons De La Vie
36. Femme Tu Es Liberee

ANNUAL 70 DAYS PRAYER AND FASTING PUBLICATIONS

1. Prayers That Bring Miracles
2. Let God Answer By Fire
3. Prayers To Mount With Wings As Eagles
4. Prayers That Bring Explosive Increase
5. Prayers For Open Heavens
6. Prayers To Make You Fulfill Your Divine Destiny
7. Prayers That Make God To Answer And Fight By Fire
8. Prayers That Bring Unchallengeable Victory And Breakthrough Rainfall Bombardments
9. Prayers That Bring Dominion Prosperity And Uncommon Success
10. Prayers That Bring Power And Overflowing Progress
11. Prayers That Bring Laughter And Enlargement Breakthroughs
12. Prayers That Bring Uncommon Favour And Breakthroughs
13. Prayers That Bring Unprecedented Greatness And Unmatchable Increase
14. Prayers That Bring Awesome Testimonies And Turn Around Breakthroughs
15. Prayers That Bring Glorious Restoration
16. Prayers That Bring Unrivaled Lifting

**The Books, Tapes and CDs (Audio and Video)
All Obtainable At:**

☞ **Battle Cry Christian Ministries**
   322, Herbert Macaulay Way, Sabo, Yaba, Lagos
   Phone: 01 8044415, 0803 304 4239

☞ **MFM International Bookshop**
   13, Olasimbo Street, Onike, Yaba, Lagos

☞ **MFM Prayer City**
   Km 12, Lagos/Ibadan Expressway

☞ **54, Akeju Street, off Shipeolu Street**
   Palmgrove, Lagos

☞ **All MFM Churches Nationwide**

☞ **IPFY Music Konnections Limited**
   48 Opebi Road, Salvation Bus Stop
   234-47194971, 234-8033056093

☞ **All Leading Christian Bookstores**

BOOK ORDER

Is there any book written by Dr. D. K. Olukoya
(General Overseer MFM Ministries)
or his wife Pastor (Mrs.) Shade Olukoya
that you would like to have?
Have you seen his/her latest books?
To place an order for this End-Time Materials,
Call : 08161229775
Battle Cry Christian Ministries... equipping the saints of God
God bless you.

ABOUT THE BOOK

I Decree an Uncommon Change is an explosive book. The Author has given us insights into the unlimited power of faith decrees. Drawing invaluable lessons from exclusive Bible passages, portraying the fact that the believer has been endowed with an irresistible power of attorney and challenging the reader to rise up to promulgate life-changing decrees, the author has sparked up a spiritual revolution in the lives of men, women and youths.

Carefully written, well researched, scripturally sound and offered in a readable form, I Decree an Uncommon Change will lead every reader to the mountain top of victory. It is backed up with a prayer programme that will produce multiple testimonies.

ABOUT THE AUTHOR

P astor (Mrs.) Shade Olukoya is the wife of the General Overseer of The Mountain of Fire and Miracles Ministries. Her life and that of the General Overseer and their son, Elijah Toluwani are living proofs that all power belongs to God. Mountain of Fire and Miracles Ministries, is a ministry devoted to absolute holiness within and without, as the greatest insecticide, and a condition for heaven is taught openly. MFM is a do-it-yourself Gospel Ministry, where your hands are trained to wage war and your fingers to do battle